A Visit to
CANADA

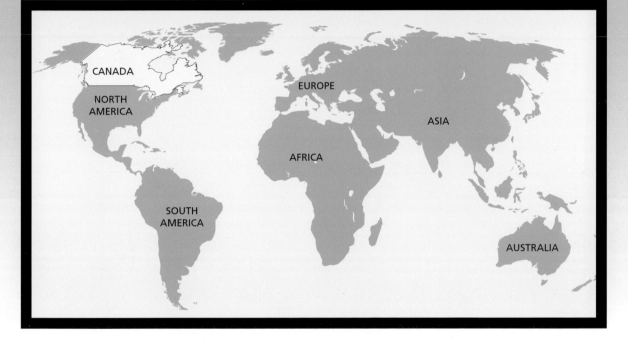

Mary Quigley

Heinemann Library
Chicago, Illinois

Designed by Sarah Figlio. Photo Research by Alan Gottlieb
Printed in China by South China Printing Company

07 06 05 04 03
10 9 8 7 6 5 4 3 2 1

Library of Congress Cataloging-in-Publication Data
Quigley, Mary, 1963-
  Canada / Mary Quigley.
      p. cm. -- (A visit to)
Summary: Introduces the land, native animals, clothing, school, work, transportation, food, arts, and celebrations of Canada.
Includes bibliographical references and index.
  ISBN 1-40340-964-1 (library binding-hardcover)
  1. Canada--Juvenile literature. 2. Canada--Social life and customs--1945---Juvenile literature. [1. Canada.] I. Title. II. Series.
F1008.2 .Qu54 2002
  971--dc21

                    2002007418

Acknowledgments
The author and publishers are grateful to the following for permission to reproduce copyright material: pp. 5, 17 Neil Hokan/Spectrum Stock; p. 6 Mark Newman/Spectrum Stock; p. 7 Robert McGouey/Spectrum Stock; p. 8 Tony Mihok/Spectrum Stock; p. 9 Jon Hicks/Corbis; p. 10 Chris Schwartz/Spectrum Stock; p. 11 Robert Estall/Corbis; p. 12 Paul Robitaille/Spectrum Stock; p. 13 Ton Freda/Visual Contact; p. 14 Jay Dickman/Corbis; p. 15 Paul A. Souders/Corbis; p. 16 Ottmar Bierwagen/Spectrum Stock; p. 18 Bob Chambers/Spectrum Stock; p. 19 Via-Rail; p. 20 Parks Canada/Pierre Saint-Jacques; p. 21 Richard T. Nowitz/Corbis; p. 22 Annie Griffiths Belt/Corbis; p. 23 Tessa MacIntosh/Spectrum Stock; p. 24 Boris Spremo/Magma Photos; p. 25 Dave Reede/First Light, Toronto; p. 26 JWE/Spectrum Stock; p. 27 Nik Wheeler/Corbis; p. 28 Marilyn "Angel" Wynn/Nativestock; p. 29 Al Seib/Cirque du Soleil Inc.

Cover photograph by Lionel Delevingne/Stock Boston

Every effort has been made to contact copyright holders of any material reproduced in this book. Any omissions will be rectified in subsequent printings if notice is given to the publisher.

Some words are shown in bold, **like this.** You can find out what they mean by looking in the glossary.

Contents

Canada

Yukon
Territory

Northwest
Territories

British
Columbia

Alberta

Saskatchewan

Manitoba

Hudson
Bay

Ontario

Quebec

Newfoundland

Prince
Edward Island

Key
- ✪ Capital
- • Landmark
- Quebec **Province Name**

Lake
Superior

Lake
Huron

Ottawa ✪

CN Tower •

Lake
Ontario

Nova
Scotia

New
Brunswick

UNITED STATES

Lake
Michigan

• Niagara Falls

Lake Erie

Atlantic Ocean

N
W   E
S

Canada is in North America. The Canadian
flag is white and red with a red maple
leaf on it. The maple leaf is the country's
national symbol.

Canada is home to people of many **cultures**. Canadians say that their country is like a mosaic. A mosaic is a work of art made of many different tiles.

Land

Canada is a very big country. There are mountains, prairies, and **rain forests**. There are snowy, frozen areas with **glaciers**. Canada has a lot of lakes and rivers.

Canada is home to many birds and animals.
People who live in Canada might see wolves,
grizzly bears, arctic foxes, beavers, moose,
and Canada geese, depending on where
they live.

Niagara Falls is a place in Canada that many people visit. Niagara Falls is shared by both Canada and the United States.

The CN Tower in Toronto, Canada, is the tallest **freestanding** building in the world. From this building, you can see for miles.

Homes

Homes in Canadian cities are very close together with small yards. Other homes are in **suburbs**. People have more room in suburbs, but they can still drive into a city. Some people live in apartments, too.

Farm families live in **rural** areas. People might have a second home, like a cottage, in the woods or by a lake. Some people live in cottages or cabins year-round.

Food

Canadians get a lot of meat, fruits, and vegetables from the land. Popular foods include salmon, beef, blueberries, and potatoes. Maple syrup is poured on pancakes. It is also made into candy.

Some restaurants serve pieces of real **icebergs** in their sodas. Canadians come from many different **ethnic** backgrounds. So, they enjoy their favorite foods from around the world.

Clothes

Canadians dress according to the weather
and what they like. Children often
wear jeans and T-shirts or sweatshirts.
They dress up for special occasions.

People wear different things for work and play. Some people wear uniforms for their jobs. The Royal Canadian Mounted Police have special uniforms they wear for parades.

Work

Some Canadians are farmers, while others are fishers. Canada is a source of wood and paper products, so many people work in the **lumber** or paper industry.

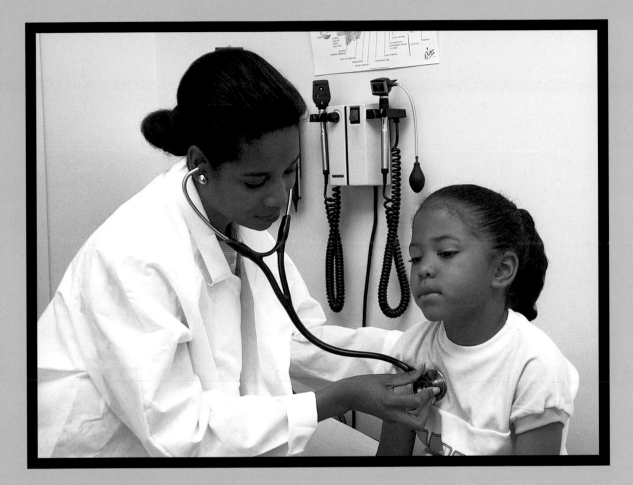

Some people provide services, such as teachers or doctors. Others work as writers, artists, or performers. Just about any job you can think of would be a job that you could find a Canadian doing.

Transportation

Many Canadians have cars. People also ride buses. Sometimes children ride buses to school. In big cities, there are subways. Subways are trains that travel underground.

There is a train that travels all the way across Canada. Many people ride this train to see the beautiful Canadian landscape.

Languag

The official languages of Canada are French and English. This is because many people came to Canada from France and England. France and England competed to **govern** areas of Canada in the past.

When you buy something in Canada, the label will have both English and French words on it. Street signs are printed in both languages, too. There are French and English channels on the TV and radio.

School

Children must go to school from the ages of
six to eighteen. Most school children are
taught to write and speak in both French and
English. There are **public** and **private** schools.

Children who live in **rural** areas might
do their lessons by mail or by computer.
After graduation they may choose to go
to a college, university, or trade school.

Free Time

Lacrosse is Canada's oldest organized sport. Native peoples were playing it long before the French and English came to Canada. Hockey is also very popular in Canada and was invented there.

People enjoy the outdoors in Canada by
camping, boating, fishing, and ice skating.
Children also like to play games, watch tel-
evision, and listen to music.

Celebrations

On July 1 every year, Canadians celebrate Canada Day. On July 1, 1867, Canada became a self-**governing** country. People enjoy barbecues, parties, and fireworks on this day.

Quebec, Canada, has a Winter Carnival.
The **mascot** is a snowman. People come
from all over to see ice **sculptures** and a
huge ice castle.

The Arts

There is a lot of art in Canada. Native peoples made totem poles. There are rock carvings and paintings that are more than 30,000 years old.

The *Cirque du Soleil*, or Circus of the Sun, is a Canadian circus with no animals. The performers wear colorful costumes and do juggling and **acrobatics**.

Fact File

Name	The word Canada means "village" or "small community."
Capital	The **capital** of Canada is Ottawa.
Language	Most people speak French and English. Many other languages are also spoken.
Population	There are more than 31 million people living in Canada.
Money	Money is called the dollar. U.S. dollars can also be used in much of Canada.
Religions	Most Canadians are Catholic or Protestant.
Products	Lumber, paper, steel, cars, coal, and food items are sent to other countries.

French Words You Can Learn

bonjour (bon-JOUR)	hello
au revoir (o-ruh-vwahr)	goodbye
oui (wee)	yes
non (nohn)	no
merci (mair-SEE)	thank you
s'il vous plait (seel-voo-PLAY)	please
un (uhn)	one
deux (deuh)	two
trois (twah)	three

Glossary

acrobatic — tricks in tumbling or on the trapeze, tightrope, or other equipment

culture — shared beliefs and traditions

ethnic — related to a group's race, nation, tribe, religion, or language

freestanding — standing alone, free of support

glacier — large mass of ice

govern — to rule a country

iceberg — large chunk of floating ice

lacrosse — sport in which goals are made by catching and tossing a ball with a netted stick

lumber — timber, logs, or wood

mascot — animal, person, or object used to represent a team or event

private — run by a church or other non-government organization

public — run by the government

rain forest — deep woods with tall trees where rain often falls

rural — countryside

sculpture — work of art shaped out of wood, stone, or other things

suburb — area of houses near a city

Index

More Books to Read

Frost, Helen. *A Look at Canada*. Mankato, Minn.: Capstone Press, Inc., 2002.

Hamilton, Janice. *Canada*. Minneapolis: Lerner Publishing Group, 1999.

Marx, David F. *Canada*. New York: Scholastic Library Publishing, 2002.